The Early Reader's Bible

A Bible to Read All by Yourself!

New Testament

AS TOLD BY V. Gilbert Beers

ILLUSTRATIONS BY Terri Steiger

ZONDERkidz™

ZONDERVAN.com/
AUTHORTRACKER
follow your favorite authors

Jesus Came to Love Us

Christ Is Born, from Luke 2 and Matthew 1

"You cannot stay here," the man said.

"I have all the people I can take."

"But where can we sleep?" Joseph asked.

"Mary is going to have a baby."

The man looked at his animals.

"You may sleep with them," he said.

"It is the only place I have."

So Mary and Joseph went to sleep with the animals.

That night Mary had a
little baby.
"We will call him Jesus,"
Joseph said.
"That is what God said
we should do."

"This baby is God's Son," said Mary.

"That is what God said."

"This baby has come to love us,"

said Mary and Joseph.

"And he has come to help us love God."

something to ask

1. Who was this little baby?

2. Why did he come?

3. Does Jesus love you?

4. Do you love Jesus?

something to do

How do you show Jesus that you love him?

11

Angels Sing to Shepherds

The Shepherds Visit Baby Jesus, from Luke 2

"Look at the sky," a shepherd said.

"It looks like it is day," said another.

"But it is night."

The shepherds were so afraid.

They did not know what it was.

"Don't be afraid," an angel said.

"I have something to tell you.

There is a new baby in town.

You should go to see him.

He is God's Son."

Then more angels came and

filled the sky.

They sang about God.

Then they went away.

"Let's go into town

and see the baby who is God's Son,"

the shepherds said.

They ran into town and went where

the angels said they should go.

How happy they were that they

could see baby Jesus!

They wanted to tell others about God's Son.

The shepherds told all the people they could find

about God's Son.

something to ask

1. Who did the shepherds see?

2. What did the angels tell the shepherds about Jesus?

3. What did the shepherds tell others?

4. Do you tell your friends about Jesus?

5. What do you tell them?

something to do

What do you tell others about Jesus?

He loves us.

He is my friend.

He wants to be your friend, too.

He wants you to live for him.

He will help you live in God's home in heaven.

What other things do you tell about Jesus?

The Wise Men Give Their Best

Gifts for Baby Jesus, from Matthew 2

"Look at the star," a wise man said.

"I see it," said another.

"We must follow that star.

It will take us to a new king."

21

The wise men knew that
this king was a special king.
He was only a little baby now.
But God had sent him.
The wise men went on camels.
They took their best gifts
to give to the baby king.
On and on they went for many
days, following the star.

One day the star stopped.

It stopped over the town of Bethlehem.

"This is the place," the wise men said.

"The baby king is here."

The wise men went to see Jesus.

They gave him their best gifts.

They were happy that the star

had led them to Jesus.

something to ask

1. What led the wise men to Jesus?

2. What did they give him?

3. Do you give Jesus your best gifts?

something to do

Which of these gifts can you give Jesus?

Jesus' Happy Family

The Childhood of Jesus, from Luke 2

"Will you help me?" Joseph asked.

Jesus was happy to help Joseph.

Joseph made many good things.

He made things from wood.

Joseph was a carpenter.

Jesus was a carpenter, too.

He helped Joseph make things from wood.

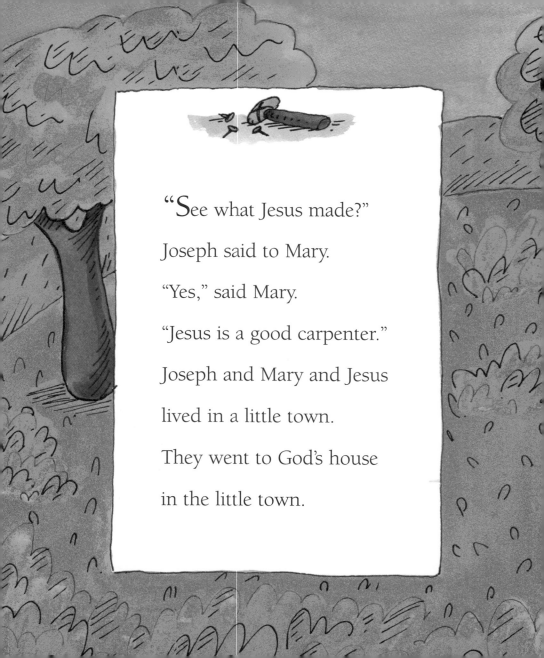

"See what Jesus made?"
Joseph said to Mary.

"Yes," said Mary.

"Jesus is a good carpenter."
Joseph and Mary and Jesus
lived in a little town.
They went to God's house
in the little town.

They liked to hear God's Word.

They liked to talk to God there.

And they liked to talk to God's people.

"They are a happy family," people said.

"They do good work with wood.

And they do good work for God, too."

something to ask

1. What work did Joseph do?

2. How did Jesus help him?

3. Do good helpers make happy families?

4. Are you a good helper?

5. How can you help your family to be happy?

something to do

Which of these will help your family be happy?

Which will not help your family be happy?

Jesus Pleases God

The Temptation of Christ, from Matthew 4

Jesus grew and became a man.

One day Jesus went away from his town.

He wanted to be alone.

Jesus talked to God for many days.

Then Satan came to see Jesus.

Jesus had not had food for a long time.

"You can make food from those rocks,"

Satan said. He was tempting Jesus.

But Jesus knew that he must not do
what Satan said.

"I must do what God tells me," said Jesus.

Satan asked Jesus three times to do
something that God would not like.

But Jesus would not do what Satan said.

"I must please God," Jesus told Satan.

39

Satan saw that he could
not get Jesus
to do what he wanted.
So Satan went away.
God was very pleased.
Jesus would not do what
Satan said.

something to ask

1. What did Satan want Jesus to do?

2. But what did Jesus do?

3. What kinds of things does Satan want you to do?

4. What should you do?

something to do

What should you do when you are tempted
to do bad things?

Do what you want?

Ask a friend to help you?

Ask God to help you?

Ask Mother or
Father to help you?

God's House

Jesus Drives Out the Money-Changers, from John 2

Jesus liked to go to God's house.

He liked to talk to God there.

He liked to be with God's people.

But Jesus did not like

what some men were doing.

They were not talking with God.

They were not talking with God's people.

These men sold animals in God's house.

These men liked to cheat.

They liked to steal, too.

"You are not doing what you

should do

in God's house," Jesus said.

"You must get out!"

Jesus made these men

get out of God's house.

God's house is not a place to cheat

and steal," said Jesus.

"We should go to God's house to

be with him.

We should talk to God in his house.

We should talk with God's people, too.

something to ask

1. What should people do in God's house?

2. What were the men doing there?

3. What did Jesus tell them to do?

4. What do YOU do when you go to God's house?

5. What should you do?

something to do

Who will you find in God's house?

God?

God's friends?

Your friends who love God?

Others who love God?

What Should I Do in God's House?

Jesus Reads from the Scriptures, from Luke 4

"Look who is here!" some people said.

All the people looked. Jesus was coming.

He was coming into God's house.

Jesus went up where the people could see him.

Then he looked at God's Word.

Jesus began to read what God's Word said.

The boys and girls were quiet.

The mothers and fathers were quiet, too.

Jesus told them about God's Son.

He told them what God's Word said about him.

"I am God's Son," he told them.

"No," some of the people said.

"You are not God's Son."

The people did not like what
Jesus said.

They took him away from God's
house. They tried to kill him.

But Jesus went away from them.

These people made Jesus sad.

They did not do what they
should with God's Son.

something to ask

1. What did Jesus do in God's house?

2. What did the people do?

3. What should people do with God's Son in God's house?

something to do

What things should you do in God's house?

A Friend Who Was Sick

Jesus Heals a Paralytic, from Mark 2

"Is Jesus in the house?" some men asked.

"Yes, but you cannot get in," said others.

"There are too many people."

"Our friend is sick," said the men,

"and Jesus can make him well."

But the men could not get into the house.

There were people here and people there.

The men could not get through.

"Then we will go in another way," they said.

So they let their friend down through the roof.

"Please help our friend," they said to Jesus. "He is sick."

Jesus was happy to help their sick friend.

"Get up," said Jesus. "You are well."

The man got up. He was not sick now.

He was so happy.

"Thank you! Thank you!" he said.

The men were happy, too.

Their friend did not hurt now.

Jesus had made him well.

something to ask

1. What did the sick man's friends do?

2. How did Jesus help?

3. How can Jesus help you when you hurt?

4. Will you ask him to help you?

something to do

What can you do for a friend when he hurts?

Which of these would you do?

Ask God to help him?

Tell him you are his friend?

Ask others to help him?

Tell him how bad he is?

Tell him how good you are?

Doing God's Work

Jesus Calls Matthew, from Matthew 9

Matthew had good work.

He had all the money he wanted.

And people did what he told them to do.

But Matthew was not happy.

He knew that he did not please God in his work.

One day Jesus came to see Matthew.

"Matthew," Jesus said,

"come with me and work for me."

Matthew looked at Jesus.

Jesus would not pay him for his work.

He would not make much money.

People would not do what he said.

He would have to do what Jesus said.

"What should I do?" Matthew asked.

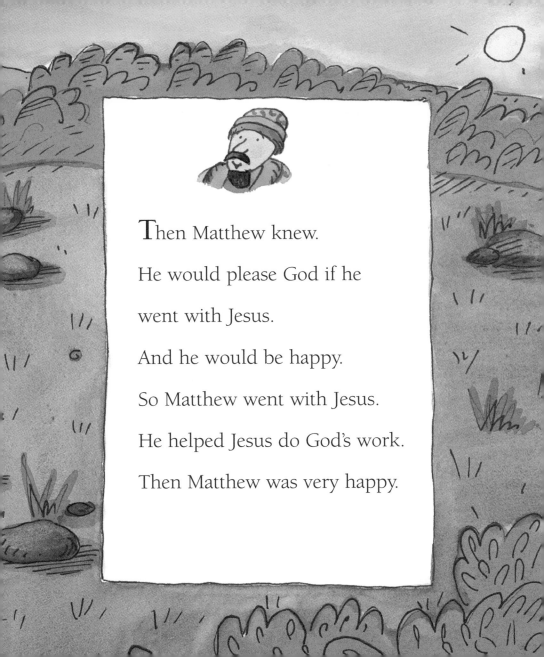

Then Matthew knew.

He would please God if he

went with Jesus.

And he would be happy.

So Matthew went with Jesus.

He helped Jesus do God's work.

Then Matthew was very happy.

something to ask

1. Why was Matthew not happy?

2. What helped him become happy?

3. What can make YOU happy?

4. Will you do these things?

something to do

What will make you happy:

When you do what you want?

When you do what your friends tell you to do?

When you do what God wants?

When you do what Mother and Father ask you?

Look What Jesus Can do!

Jesus Stills a Storm, from Luke 8

"Come with me," said Jesus.

"Where?" asked his friends.

"To the other side of the lake," Jesus said.

Jesus and his friends got into their boat.

These friends liked to go with Jesus.

They knew that Jesus did good things for God.

They knew that God helped Jesus do these things.

Soon the boat was out on

the water.

Then the wind started to blow.

Faster and faster went the wind.

The boat went up and down on

the water.

Jesus' friends were so afraid.

"Help us!" they said to Jesus.

"The boat is going down!"

Jesus looked at the wind blowing on the water.

"Stop!" he said.

The wind stopped blowing.

The water stopped going up and down.

And the boat stopped going up and down.

"Did you see that?" one of Jesus' friends said.

The others looked at Jesus.

"Only God's Son could do that," they said.

something to ask

1. Who told the wind what to do?

2. How could he do that?

3. Do you know anyone who can do that?

4. Can you do that?

5. Do you do what Jesus wants, too?

something to do

Which of these should do what Jesus says to do?

Can a Man Do This?

Jesus Heals a Little Girl, from Mark 5

"Please come to my house," Jairus said.

"My little girl is going to die."

Jesus went with Jairus.

But it took a long time to get to his house.

People were here.

People were there.

The people all wanted to see Jesus.

Then someone came from
Jairus' house and said,
"Your little girl has died."
Jairus was so sad, but Jesus
said, "Don't be afraid."
Jesus and Jairus went into the
house. People were crying.
"Don't be sad," said Jesus.
"The little girl is sleeping."

Some people laughed at Jesus.

"Get out of this house," Jesus said to them.

So the people who laughed went away.

Jesus looked at the girl.

"Get up, little girl!" he said to her.

The little girl got up.

"Give her something to eat," said Jesus.

Jairus and the girl's mother were so happy.

"Can a man do this?" they asked.

"Jesus must be God's Son!"

something to ask

1. What did Jesus do for the girl?

2. Can a man do this?

3. Who is Jesus?

4. What book tells you about Jesus?

something to do

Which of these people did what Jesus said?

Jairus?

The little girl?

The people in
Jairus' house?

Do you?

A Boy Shares His Lunch

Jesus Feeds the Five Thousand, from Matthew 14

"Here are five pieces of bread

and two fish for your lunch," a mother said.

The boy was happy.

He was going to see Jesus.

So were some of his friends.

The boy took his lunch. He ran with his friends.

At last they saw Jesus.

There were many other people there, too.

Jesus said many good things.

The boy and his friends listened.

Then Jesus stopped talking.

Some men came to the boy.

"May we have your lunch?" they

asked. "Jesus wants it."

The boy took his lunch to Jesus.

He was happy to give Jesus

his lunch.

The boy and his friends watched.

But Jesus did not eat the lunch.

He broke it into many pieces.

He gave the pieces to the people.

Soon all the people had as much

to eat as they wanted.

Jesus smiled at the boy and his friends.

"Thank you for your lunch," he said.

The boy smiled, too.

Then he sat near Jesus and ate

some bread and fish.

something to ask

1. What was in the boy's lunch?

2. What did Jesus do with it?

3. Was the boy happy to share his lunch with Jesus?

4. Would you like to share something with Jesus?

something to do

What could you share with Jesus?

Talk with Mother or Father about this.

Walking on Water

Jesus Walks on the Sea of Galilee, from Mark 6

"It is time for you to go home," Jesus said.

"Will you come with us?" his friends asked.

"Not now," said Jesus.

Jesus' friends got into their boat.

They went out on the water to go home.

Soon it was night.

The wind began to blow hard.

The water went up and down.

They worked and worked to
get the boat home.

Suddenly all of them stopped.

"Look," they said.

"Who is that walking on
the water?"

The men were afraid.

"It is a ghost!" they said.

"No, I am not a ghost,"

the man on the water said.

"It is Jesus!" said his friends.

They were so happy that it was Jesus.

"But how can he do that?" someone asked.

"Only God's Son can do things like that,"

said others. "Jesus is God's Son."

something to ask

1. Can your friends walk on water?

2. Can you?

3. Who did walk on water?

4. How could he do this?

5. Do you love God's Son?

6. Will you talk to him now?

something to do

Did God make this?

And this?

And this?

What other work can he do?

What other things did he make?

God Talks about His Son

The Transfiguration of Christ, from Matthew 17

Jesus and some friends walked up and up and up.

They went up a tall mountain.

"Why are we here?" said one friend to the other.

"We do not know," he said, "but Jesus knows."

Then Jesus' face began to shine.

His clothes began to shine, too.

Jesus' friends were so afraid.

Then two men came to be with Jesus.

"Look at those men," said Jesus' friends.

"They lived a long time ago."

Then a big cloud came over all of them.

"This is my Son," someone said.

"Do what he says."

It was God who said this.

Jesus' friends were afraid,

so they fell down by Jesus.

When they got up,

there was no one there—

no one but Jesus.

"God said that,"

said Jesus' friends.

"God said that Jesus is his Son."

Now they knew that Jesus

was God's Son.

something to ask

1. What did God say about Jesus?

2. Who was with Jesus then?

3. What can you do to please Jesus?

4. Will you do one thing for Jesus soon?

something to do

Who said that Jesus was God's Son?

Jesus did.　　　So did his friends.　　　So did God.

What do you say?

A Man Who Did Not Say Thank You

The Parable of the Rich Fool, from Luke 12

There was a man who was very rich.

He had a farm. He had big barns.

He had houses. He had money.

The man had so many things!

He did not know what to do with all his things.

"I will make bigger barns," the man said.

"I will make them bigger and bigger."

The man loved his things

more than he loved God.

He did not thank God for them.

He did not give anything away.

"These are my things." he said.

"I want them all."

But God said, "It is time for

you to die. Then others will

have all your things."

The man did not like to hear this.

But what could he do?

That night he died.

Then others had all his things.

God gives us many good things.

We should give our love to him.

And we should thank him

for the things he gives to us.

something to ask

1. Was this man rich or poor?

2. Did he want to share his things?

3. What happened to the man?

4. What things did he take with him when he died?

something to do

How can you say thank you to God?

"Thank you for your good things."

"I will do my best for you."

"I will give good things to you."

"I will share with others."

"I will tell a friend about you."

"I will love you."

The Good Shepherd

The Parable of the Lost Sheep, from Luke 15

One day Jesus told his friends about a sheep.

It was a sheep that ran away.

The sheep went far away from the others.

It could not find the way home. It was lost!

The shepherd looked at

his sheep.

He saw that one sheep

was gone.

He loved that sheep,

and he wanted to find it.

So he left his other sheep.

He went far away from home

looking for his lost sheep.

The shepherd looked and looked

for his sheep. Then he found it.

The shepherd took the sheep into his arms.

Then he took the sheep to his home.

Jesus said that we are like the sheep.

We are far away from God.

But Jesus came to find us.

He loves us.

And he helps us find the way

to God's home in heaven.

something to ask

1. What did the sheep do?

   How did it get lost?

2. What did the shepherd do?

3. How are we like the sheep?

4. What does Jesus help us do?

something to do

How can you help your family to be happy?

Jesus and the Children

Children Come to Christ, from Mark 10

"What do you want?"

some of Jesus' friends asked.

"We want to have our children see Jesus,"

said the mothers and fathers.

"You cannot do that," said Jesus' friends.

"Why not?" asked the mothers and fathers.

"Jesus has too many things to do,"

said his friends. "That's why."

Then Jesus came to them.

"What is the matter?" he asked.

"Your friends will not let our children see you,"
said the mothers and fathers.

Jesus' friends said, "We told them that you
were doing other things."

"Do not tell the children to stay away from me,"
said Jesus.

"They show others how to come to me."

Then Jesus had the children

come to see him.

He told them many things.

He told them how much

God loved them.

"Do you love us, too?"

the children asked.

"Yes," said Jesus.

"And I want you to love me."

something to ask

1. Did Jesus tell the children to go away?

2. Are children important to Jesus?

3. Does Jesus love children?
   How do you know?

4. How can you show Jesus that
   you love him?

something to do

Which kinds of children does Jesus love?

A Man Who Wanted to See

Jesus Heals a Blind Man, from Luke 18

One day Jesus was going into a town.

A poor man sat by the road.

He wanted someone to help him.

The man could not see.

He could not work.

Then Jesus came by.

"Help me," the man said to Jesus.

"Help me! Help me! Help me!"

"Stop that!" some people said.

But the man did not stop.

"Have him come here," said Jesus.

So some men helped bring him to Jesus.

"What do you want?" Jesus asked.

"I want to see," said the man.

"Then you will see," said Jesus.

At once the man could see.

He was so happy.

He could see trees.

He could see people.

And he could see Jesus.

"Thank you!" the man said.

Then the man went with Jesus
to help him do his work.

He loved Jesus very much, and
he knew that Jesus loved him.

something to ask

1. What did the poor man want?

2. What did Jesus do for him?

3. Does Jesus love poor people?

4. How do you know?

5. Do you love poor people, too?

6. What can you do for them?

something to do

Which of these will help you most?

Which will make you the most happy?

Finding a Friend

Zacchaeus and Jesus, from Luke 19

Zacchaeus was sad. He wanted friends.

But no one wanted to be his friend.

"Zacchaeus cheats," some said.

"Zacchaeus steals," said others.

One day Zacchaeus saw Jesus.

"I want Jesus to be my friend," he said.

The people laughed. "Jesus is a good Man,"

they said. "He will not be your friend."

There were people all around Jesus.

Zacchaeus wanted to see Jesus.

But Zacchaeus was a little man.

He could not get through the crowds.

"I will climb that big tree and see Jesus," he said.

So Zacchaeus climbed the big tree.

Jesus stopped under the tree and looked up.

There was Zacchaeus.

"Come down," said Jesus.

"I want to go to your house.

I want to be your friend."

Zaccheus was so happy.

He gave Jesus good things to eat.

"I'm sorry that I cheated," he said.

Jesus smiled at Zaccheus.

"I forgive you," he said.

Zaccheus was happy.

He had a new friend.

And Jesus is the best Friend of all.

something to ask

1. Why did Zacchaeus have no friends?

2. Who became his best friend?

3. Would you like Jesus to be your friend? Why?

something to do

Have you asked Jesus to be your friend?

Would you like to do that now?

Ask him to forgive you.

Ask him to help you please him.

Jesus on a Donkey

Christ Enters Jerusalem, from Mark 11

"I need a little donkey," said Jesus.

"It will help me do God's work."

Jesus' friends looked here. They looked there.

But they did not see a donkey.

"Where will we get a donkey?" they asked.

Jesus told his friends where to get a donkey.

He said a man would give them one.

Jesus' friends went to the man.

"May we use your donkey?" they asked.

"Yes," said the man. He was happy

that his donkey could help Jesus.

Then Jesus got on the donkey.

He went into a big town called Jerusalem.

Many people went with him to the big town.

They shouted, "Jesus is our King!"

In Jerusalem Jesus told people about God.

He told them how to please God.

He told them that he would die for them.

God had sent Jesus to do these things.

This was the work Jesus did for God.

something to ask

1. What kind of work did Jesus do for God?

2. How did the donkey help him?

3. What kind of work can you do for God?

something to do

How can these help you do God's work?

your your your

your your

Supper with Jesus

The Lord's Supper, from Matthew 26

"**W**here will we eat?" Jesus' friends asked.

Jesus told them where it would be.

They would eat at a house in Jerusalem.

So Jesus' friends went there.

They put the supper together.

Then Jesus and his twelve friends ate together.

"Eat this bread," Jesus said. "When I am gone,

you will do this again and again.

Then you will think of the way I died for you."

Jesus' friends ate the bread.

But they were sad.

They did not want Jesus to die.

"Drink from this cup," Jesus said.

"When I am gone, you will do this

again and again. Then you will think

of the way I died for you."

Jesus' friends drank from the cup. But they were sad. They did not want Jesus to die. Suddenly the friends heard someone singing. It was Jesus. Jesus' friends began to sing, too. This was a special time because Jesus was so special.

something to ask

1. Who was eating together?

2. What did Jesus give his friends? Why?

3. Who was singing?

something to do

When do you think of this special supper?

Talk with Mother or Father about this.

The Love of Jesus

The Death of Christ, from Matthew 27

"Nail that man to the cross!" someone said.

The men nailed Jesus to the cross.

Then they watched him die.

Jesus had not hurt these men.

But they were hurting him.

Jesus talked to God about these men.

"Forgive them for hurting me," he said.

These people had not seen a man like this.

They were hurting him.

But he was loving them.

"That man is God's Son," said one of them.

When Jesus died on the cross,
he showed how much he
loved them.
And he showed how much he
loves you and me.
How much does Jesus love us?
He loves us so much that he
died so we can come to God.

something to ask

1. Why did the men hurt Jesus?

2. Did he hurt them?

3. Did he love them?

4. Does Jesus love you?
   Does he forgive you?

5. Do you love him?

6. Would you like to tell him this?

something to do

How can you show Jesus that you love him?

How can you show it with each of these?

Jesus Is Alive Again!

Mary Sees the Risen Christ, from John 20

Mary was so sad.

Some men had killed Jesus.

Now Mary came to see where they had put him.

But Jesus was not there.

"Someone has taken him away," said Mary.

Mary began to cry.

Then some angels talked to Mary.

"Why are you crying?" they asked.

"Someone has taken Jesus away,"
she said.

Then Mary saw a man coming.

"Why are you crying?" he asked.

"Someone has taken Jesus away,"
she said.

"Mary!" the man said.

"Jesus!" said Mary.

Mary was so happy.

Jesus was alive again!

"I cannot stay with you," Jesus said.

"I must go back to my home in heaven."

Now Mary knew that Jesus was God's Son.

something to ask

1. Why did Mary cry?

2. Who came to see her?

3. What did he tell Mary?

4. Who is Jesus?

5. How did Mary know that Jesus was God's Son?

something to do

How do you know that Jesus is God's Son?

He did God's work.

He told others about God.

He did not do bad things.

He helped some people come
alive after they died.

He said that he was God's Son.

He came alive after some men killed him.

Telling Others about Jesus

The Church Grows, from Acts 1-8

"Go to all the world," Jesus said.

"Tell people everywhere

about what I did for them."

After Jesus said these things

he went back to heaven to stay.

Jesus' friends knew that he was God's Son.

He had died for them.

Then he had come back to live with them.

Only God's Son could do that!

They knew that Jesus showed people

the way to know God.

So they went to all the people.

They went to tell them about Jesus.

"Jesus loves you," they said.

"He wants to help you get to know God."

Some people liked what they heard. But others said,

"Go away"

Jesus' friends were happy when some people did come to love Jesus.

something to ask

1. What did Jesus ask his friends to do?

2. How did they do it?

3. Why did they do it?

4. What does he want you to do for him?

5. How can you tell others about him?

something to do

Where should you tell others about Jesus?

At your house?

At a friend's house?

Here and there
and everywhere?

A Man Hears about Jesus

Philip and the Ethiopian, from Acts 8

"Leave this town," an angel told Philip.

"Go where I tell you to go."

Philip left that town.

He went far away to the place

where the angel told him to go.

"But there are no people here," said Philip.

"How can I do God's work here?"

Then Philip saw a man coming.
The man was looking at God's
Word. "Do you know what it
says?" Philip asked.

"No," said the man. "I need
someone to help me.
Will you help me?"

"Yes," said Philip, "I will."

"God sent me here to help you."

So Philip told the man

what God's Word said.

He told the man about Jesus.

"I want to do what Jesus says,"

the man told Philip.

Philip was so happy.

Now he knew why God had sent him there.

He knew that this man

would tell many others about Jesus.

something to ask

1. What did the man want Philip to help him do?

2. Why do you want others to help you know God's Word?

3. Who can you help? What can you do to help them?

4. What can you do to know more about God's Word?

something to do

Where do you hear about Jesus?

God's Word?

Books about Jesus?

Mother
and Father?

God's house?

Friends who
love Jesus?

Brighter than the Sun

Saul's Conversion, from Acts 9

words to know

Saul
bright
Damascus
hate
person

Saul hated Jesus.

And he hated Jesus' friends.

He did not want people to follow Jesus.

Saul did not think that Jesus was God's Son.

Saul thought Jesus was dead. He said,

"Why should people follow a dead person?"

So Saul tried to hurt Jesus' friends.

One day Saul went to a city
called Damascus.

He went to hurt Jesus' friends.

But on the way, something
happened.

Suddenly the sky was bright.

It was brighter than the sun.

It was so bright that Saul fell
down.

Then someone from heaven said,

"Stop hurting me."

"Who are you?" Saul asked.

"What do you want me to do?"

He was afraid. No one from heaven

had talked to him before.

"I am Jesus," the person said. "Follow me!"

Now Saul knew that Jesus was alive.

He knew that Jesus was God's Son.

He knew that Jesus was in heaven.

He would follow Jesus as long as he lived.

something to ask

1. Why did Saul hate Jesus' friends?

2. What did he want them to do?

3. Why did he go to Damascus?

4. Who talked to him?
   What did Jesus say?

5. Why did Saul become Jesus' follower?

something to do

Have you asked Jesus,

"What would you like me to do for you?"

Would you like to ask him now?

words to know

Paul
Silas
shake
door
himself

Singing in Jail

Paul and Silas in Prison, from Acts 16

Paul and Silas were doing God's work.

They were telling people that Jesus is God's Son.

They were helping people love Jesus.

But some men did not like that.

They hated Jesus. They hated Jesus' friends, too.

"Put those men in jail!" they shouted.

"They are doing bad things."

Some men put Paul and Silas in
jail. That night Paul and Silas
began to sing songs about God.
Suddenly the jail began to shake.
The door of the jail broke.
The man at the jail was afraid
that someone would hurt him
if Paul and Silas got away.
So he tried to kill himself.

"Stop," said Paul. "We are all here."

Now the man knew that God took care

of Paul and Silas.

"I want Jesus to forgive me," he said.

"I want to love Jesus and follow him.

What should I do?"

"Ask Jesus to forgive you," said Paul

So the man did. He prayed to Jesus.

His family became Jesus' friends, too.

They were all happy.

Do you think they sang happy songs, too?

something to ask

1. Why did men put Paul and
   Silas in jail?

2. What did they do in jail?

3. What do you do when you get hurt?
   Do you sing, or do you say bad things?

4. What good thing happened to the
   man at the jail?

something to do

When should we sing songs about God?

When things go well?

When people hurt me?

When people help me?

When I am happy?

When I am not happy?

Paul Is a Brave Helper

Paul's Shipwreck, from Acts 27

"What can we do?" the people cried.

The wind made their boat go here and there.

The rain came down on them.

They were in a bad storm.

There was nothing they could do.

"We will all be killed!" they said.

"No," said Paul, "God told me that no one will be killed." Then Paul told them about God. He told them how God would help them.

Paul was very brave.

He knew that God was with them.

The storm made the boat

sink under the water.

But the people did not go down with it.

God helped them get to the land.

Then the people were happy that

Paul was with them.

They were happy that he was

God's brave helper.

something to ask

1. What did Paul do when a storm came?

2. How was he brave when others
   were afraid?

3. How was this doing God's work?

4. How can you be brave when others
   are afraid?

something to do

How are these people helping others
who are afraid?

Helping a Friend

Paul and Onesimus, from the Book of Philemon

Onesimus had run away.

Onesimus had worked for Philemon.

But he had run away from Philemon.

Onesimus had taken some

of Philemon's things, too.

Onesimus ran away to a big town.

Paul saw Onesimus in the big
town. He told him about Jesus.
Onesimus began to love Jesus.
Then he wanted to go back
home to Philemon.
He wanted Philemon to take
him back.
He wanted Philemon to love him
and not hurt him.

So Paul wrote to Philemon for Onesimus.

"Philemon," Paul said,

"Onesimus loves Jesus now.

He wants to do what is right.

Will you take him back to work for you?"

Onesimus was happy to have a friend like Paul.

He was happy that Paul helped him do

what was right.

something to ask

1. What did Onesimus do?

2. Why did he want to go back
   to Philemon?

3. How did Paul help Onesimus?

4. What do you think Philemon did?

5. How can you help others do what
   they should for God?

something to do

How can you help a friend do what is right?

Talk to him?

Make fun of him?

Work with him?

Tell others bad things about him?

Ask God to help him?

Story List

Basic Word List

Most of the words on this basic word list have come from standard word lists used in public school early reader books. If your child is learning to read in a public or private school, he or she should be familiar with most of these basic words. This will depend, of course, on the specific school reading material used.

With each Bible story reading you will find no more than five new words not found on the basic list. These words are accumulated so that a new word used in one reading never appears as a new word in subsequent readings.

a	by	give	know	now	some
about	call	go	last	of	someone
afraid	came	good	laugh	on	something
after	can	got	led	one	son
all	children	had	let	only	song
am	come	happen	like	other	soon
an	could	happy	little	our	stay
and	day	has	live	out	steal
animal	did	have	long	over	stop
another	do	he	look	people	take
are	does	hear	love	please	talk
around	don't	help	made	put	tall
as	down	here	make	rain	tell
ask	eat	him	man	ran	than
at	far	his	many	road	thank
ate	fast	home	may	run	that
away	father	house	me	sad	the
baby	fell	how	men	said	their
bad	find	hurt	more	sang	them
be	fish	I	mother	sat	then
became	food	in	much	saw	there
began	for	into	must	see	these
best	friend	is	my	sent	they
big	from	it	new	should	thing
boat	gave	kill	night	show	this
boy	get	king	no	sing	those
but	girl	knew	not	so	through

time	tree	want	went	why	would
to	tried	was	were	will	yes
told	up	water	what	wind	you
too	us	way	when	with	your
took	very	we	where	word	
town	walk	well	who	work	

New Word List

The following is a cumulative list of the new words used in the Bible readings. No more than five new words are used in any story, and usually a smaller number is used.

Because these stories are from the Bible, many of the new words are names of Bible people or places. These words are first steps in acquainting your child with the people and places of the bible.

alive	cup	hard	Matthew	quiet	special
alone	Damascus	hate	money	read	stars
angel	dead	heard	most	right	suddenly
arm	donkey	himself	mountain	rock	supper
barn	door	important	nail	roof	tempt
Bethlehem	drank	jail	need	Satan	three
bread	everywhere	Jairus	nothing	Saul	together
bright	face	Jerusalem	obey	shake	twelve
bring	family	Jesus	once	sheep	under
broke	farm	Joseph	Onesimus	shepherd	use
camel	fill	lake	Paul	shine	wise
carpenter	five	leave	pay	shout	wood
cheat	follow	left	person	sick	wrote
climb	forgive	listen	Philemon	Silas	Zacchaeus
clothes	ghost	lost	Philip	sink	
cross	gift	lunch	piece	sky	
crowd	God	Mary	place	sleep	
cry	grew	matter	poor	smile	

Hardcover · 6 1/3" x 7 5/16"
ISBN 0-310-70139-2

Available at your local bookstore!

A Bible to read all by yourself!

Beginning readers will love the feeling of accomplishment when they read *The Early Reader's Bible* on their own. Sixty-four easy-to-read Bible stories based on public school word lists introduce new vocabulary words—including Bible vocabulary. Filled with colorful illustrations, stimulating questions, and real-life applications, this Bible storybook is sure to be a favorite!

ZONDERkidz™
INSPIRING YOUNG LIVES.